Growing and Changing

Module B

Growing and Changing

Changes are going on all around you. Everything changes! Living things change as they grow. Even the land and water change.

Chapter 1

Growing Up

Growing is changing. How do you think you will look when you grow up? Page **B 4**

Chapter 2
How Animals Grow
Where did that caterpillar go? Some animals go through many changes as they grow.
Page **B 24**

Chapter 3
Changing Things
Don't throw that away! Recycle it! Page **B 42**

Chapter 1

11/12/16

Growing Up

Do you like to look at your baby pictures? Think of how small you were! Why are baby pictures fun to look at?

You know that you do not look like a baby anymore. You have changed. You have more teeth. You have grown. How else have you changed?

What changes do you see?

1. Bring your baby picture and your first grade picture to school.
2. Fold a piece of paper in half. Tape one picture on each side.
3. Write how you looked as a baby.
4. Write how you look now.
5. **Tell about it.** Tell ways you have changed.

Ask me what else I want to find out about growing and changing.

How did you change in one year?

Think about how glad you are to be in first grade. Why are you so happy?

You can do many things now that you could not do last year. Maybe you take a bus to school this year. What other changes have happened to you since kindergarten? How have the children in the pictures changed since last year?

Checkpoint

Write a story. Tell what you do now that you could not do in kindergarten.

"Last year it was hard to sit quietly. Now I can!"

"Last year I could not subtract numbers, but now I can!"

Which teeth have you lost?

Smile! It is school picture day. This picture will look different from your picture taken last year. Your first teeth may be coming out. Larger permanent teeth will take their place.

You will need:

 crayons

 paper

 mirror

Find out about it.

1 Look at your teeth in the mirror.

2 Find the places where teeth are missing. Point to those teeth on the chart.

3 Find any loose teeth. Point to those teeth on the chart.

Write about it.

Make a chart like this one. Color the
missing teeth blue. Color the loose teeth red.

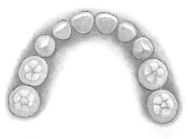 upper
teeth

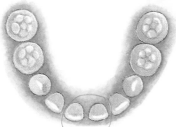 lower
teeth

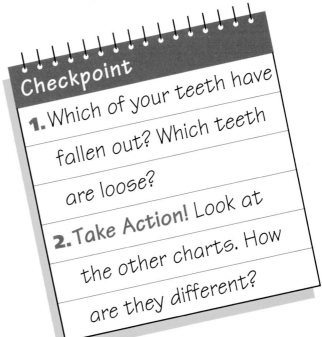

Checkpoint

1. Which of your teeth have
fallen out? Which teeth
are loose?

2. Take Action! Look at
the other charts. How
are they different?

How do people grow and change?

How will you change as you grow older? As you grow, your size and shape change. You will be able to do new things. You will learn more about getting along with people.

When you are grown up, you will be an adult. How do you think you will look and act as an adult?

Tell about growing up.

You will need:  pictures

1. Ask an adult for pictures of herself or himself. The pictures should show the person as a baby, a child, and an adult.
2. Bring the pictures to class.
3. Put the pictures in order. Start with the baby picture.
4. Tell how the person changed.

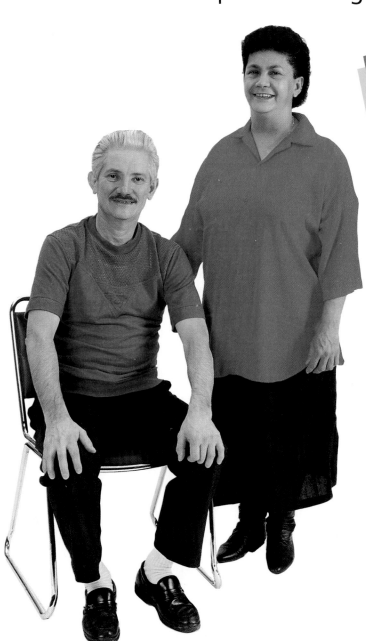

Checkpoint

Draw a picture of how you think you will look when you grow up. Tell about your picture.

What can help you grow?

As you grow, your body needs certain things. These things keep you healthy. Look at the pictures. Now read about four things that help you grow and be healthy.

Exercise helps you. When you play hard, you get exercise. What games do you play that are good exercise?

Rest helps you. When you sit or sleep you get rest. How do you feel when you do not get enough rest?

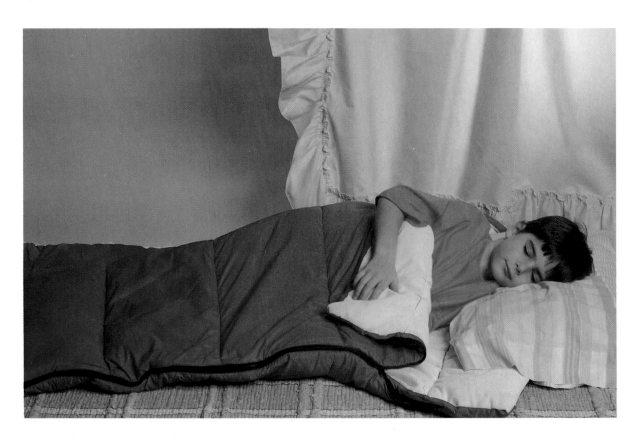

Keeping clean helps you. When you wash you get rid of germs that can make you sick. How do you keep clean?

Food helps you. Some foods are better for you than other foods. What are some foods that help you grow and be healthy?

Checkpoint

Make a poster. Show yourself doing the four things that help you grow and be healthy.

What kinds of foods help you grow?

fats, oils, sweets

milk, yogurt, cheese

meat, fish, dry beans and peas, eggs, nuts

vegetables

fruits

cereal, bread, rice, pasta

Do you think your favorite foods help you grow? Different kinds of food help you grow and be healthy. The chart above can help you decide which foods are better for you. You need more of the foods at the bottom of the chart. You need less of the foods near the top.

Make a food chart.

You will need: glue  paper ✂ scissors

 magazines

1. Look through the magazines.
2. Cut out pictures of different kinds of food.
3. Copy the chart.
4. Glue your pictures in the correct place on the chart.

Checkpoint

Tell why you put the pictures where you did.

What happens to the food you eat?

It's time for lunch! You are very hungry. But what happens to the food you eat? Your body breaks down food and changes it. Then the food can be used by your body.

The way your body changes food is called **digestion.** Digestion starts in your mouth. Teeth break food into small pieces. As you chew, a liquid called **saliva** mixes with food.

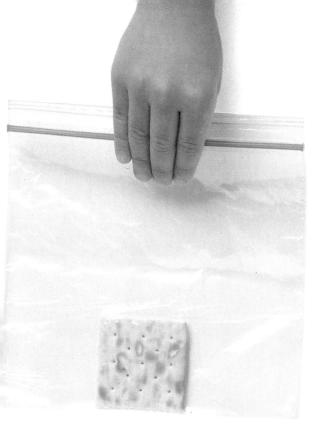

12-14-16

Observe what happens when food is chewed.

You will need: 2 crackers water

 2 plastic bags

1. Put 1 cracker into a bag.
2. Put the second cracker into the other bag. Break the cracker into small pieces.
3. Add water to both bags. Seal the bags.
4. Shake each bag 10 times.
5. Look at the 2 crackers. How are they different?

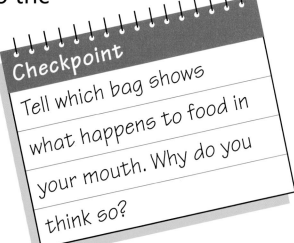

Checkpoint

Tell which bag shows what happens to food in your mouth. Why do you think so?

What happens after you swallow?

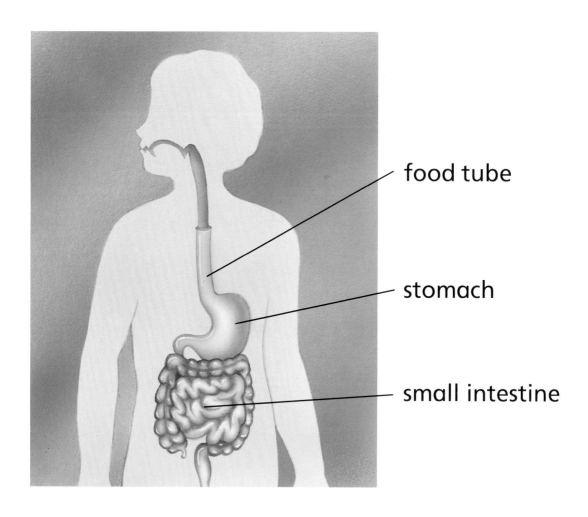

food tube

stomach

small intestine

After you swallow, food is changed more and more. First, it goes down your **food tube** into your stomach. Your **stomach** squeezes food and changes it into a soupy liquid. Then the liquid food moves into the small intestine. Your **small intestine** breaks down the liquid food more. Now the food can be used by your body.

Show the body parts that digest food.

You will need:  mural paper ✏ paper towel tube
🎈 balloon ◯ string 🧴 glue ✏ crayon

1. Have your partner trace your outline on the paper.
2. Make a model of the body parts that digest food. Glue the tube, balloon, and string on your outline.
3. Tell which body part looks like a tube. Tell which body part looks like a balloon. Which body part looks like string?

Checkpoint

Use your model to show how food moves through the body. Tell how food changes.

How long does it take to digest food?

Digestion can take a long time. The drawing shows about how long food stays in each part of the body.

1. Look at the drawing. Food takes about 8 seconds to go down the food tube. How long does food stay in the stomach? How long does it stay in the small intestine?

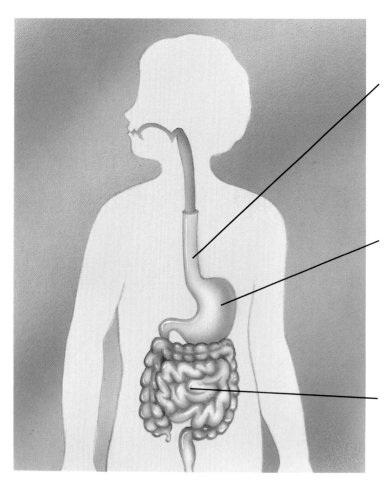

Food is in the food tube about 8 seconds.

Food is in the stomach about 1 to 4 hours.

Food is in the small intestine about 4 hours.

2. Draw a chart like this one.

part of the body	time
food tube	about 8 seconds
stomach	
small intestine	

3. The chart shows about how long food stays in the food tube. On your chart write how long food stays in the stomach. Write how long food stays in the small intestine.

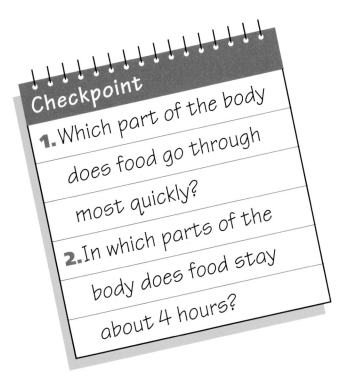

Checkpoint

1. Which part of the body does food go through most quickly?

2. In which parts of the body does food stay about 4 hours?

What did you learn?

My, have you grown! Think of how you have changed. What things help you grow and change? Share what you know by making a book about growing up.

You will need: paper crayons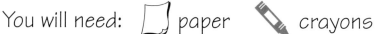

 pencil

Make a book.

1. Draw a picture of some things you did when you were little.
2. Make a picture of something you will do this year.
3. Draw pictures of you doing the four things that help you grow and be healthy.
4. Draw the parts of the body that help digest your food.
5. Write about your pictures.
6. Make a front and back cover for your book.
7. Put all of your pages together.

HereIAM.

me

Chapter 2

How Animals Grow

You know that you are growing and changing in many ways. What other things grow and change?

Think about the animals where you live. Maybe you see birds and spiders. Maybe your neighbor has a dog or a cat. All of these animals grow and change. Do animals grow and change in the same ways? Let's find out.

Does a mealworm grow?

1. Place a mealworm on a paper.
2. Mark the beginning and the end of the mealworm. Write day 1 next to it.
3. Do this every 2 days.
4. **Tell about it.** Tell if a mealworm grows. How do you know?

Ask me what else I want to find out about how animals grow and change.

What do animals need to grow?

Animals need four things to live and to grow. One thing animals need is food. Where do you think animals get their food?

Another thing animals need is water. Where might animals find water? Animals also need air and a place to live. You can make a home for mealworms.

Make a home for mealworms.

You will need: tape apple slice oatmeal

 mealworms plastic container with lid

1. Put some oatmeal in the container.
2. Place an apple slice inside the container.
3. Put mealworms into the container and tape on the lid.
4. Put the home in a warm place away from sunlight.

Checkpoint

Tell how the home has the four things the mealworm needs to live.

How do insects change?

Animals called insects hatch from eggs. Some baby insects look much like the adult insect. One of these insects is the grasshopper.

Some insects change shape as they grow. A mealworm is a **larva.** It will change into a beetle. What shape is the larva? How is the pupa different from the larva? What does the adult look like?

Checkpoint

Tell how a grasshopper changes as it grows. Draw pictures to show how a mealworm changes.

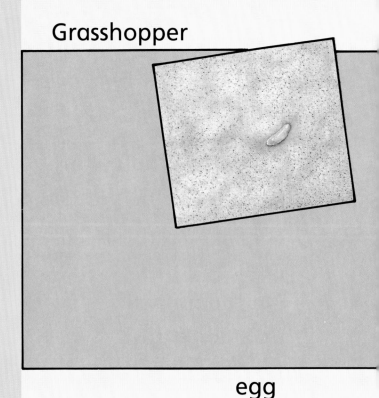

Grasshopper

egg

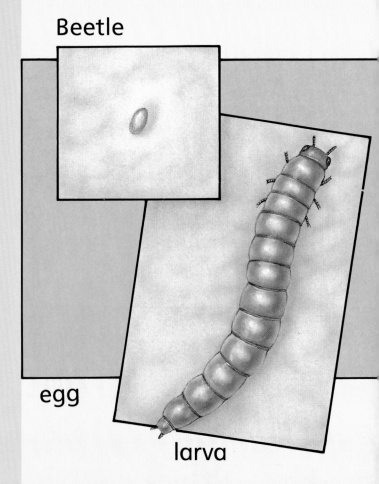

Beetle

egg

larva

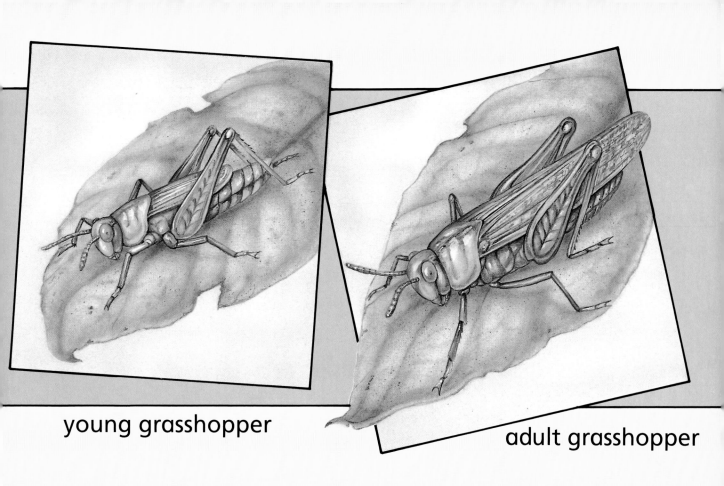

young grasshopper

adult grasshopper

pupa

adult beetle

How do mealworms change?

You found out how mealworms change as they grow. Now let's look at those changes.

You will need:

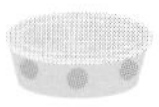

mealworm home

mealworms

hand lens

crayons

Find out about it.

1 Take the lid off the mealworm home.

2 Look at the mealworms with the hand lens.

3 Watch the mealworms for 14 days. Try to find a pupa. Look for adult beetles. Look at the color, size, and shape of each.

Write about it.

Make a chart like this one. Write down or draw the changes in the mealworms.

day	how mealworms look
1	
2	

Checkpoint

1. How did the mealworms change?

2. What change is the most surprising?

3. Take Action! Make a model of a mealworm.

How does a butterfly change?

A butterfly is another insect that changes as it grows. A butterfly hatches from an egg. The larva of a butterfly is called a caterpillar. A caterpillar eats and grows. It changes into a **pupa.** A covering forms around the pupa. Inside the covering, the pupa changes into a butterfly. The butterfly breaks open the covering and crawls out. The butterfly is the adult insect.

caterpillar

pupa

Show how a caterpillar changes into a butterfly.

You will need: cover goggles construction paper modeling clay scissors pipe cleaners

1. Shape the clay into a caterpillar.
2. Shape your caterpillar to show how it changes into a pupa.
3. Show how the pupa changes into a butterfly. Put paper wings on the butterfly.
4. Use pipe cleaners for the antennas and legs.

butterfly

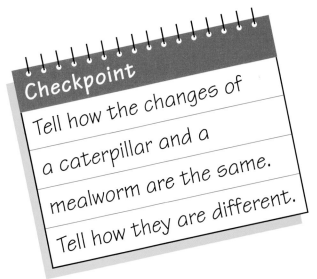

Checkpoint

Tell how the changes of a caterpillar and a mealworm are the same. Tell how they are different.

What other animals hatch from eggs?

You learned that insects hatch from eggs. Many other animals also hatch from eggs.

These robins, like other birds, hatch from eggs. A baby bird does not change much as it grows. It looks a lot like its parents. But a baby bird cannot fly. As the bird grows, its feathers change. Most adult birds can fly.

A frog is another animal that hatches from an egg. A baby frog is called a tadpole. Tadpoles change as they grow. Look at the picture. How does the tadpole change?

Checkpoint

Draw two animals that hatch from eggs.

eggs

adult frog

tadpoles

How do some animals grow and change?

Some animals do not hatch from eggs. Some animals grow inside their mother until they are born. Cats and dogs are animals that are born.

The pictures show how rabbits grow and change after they are born. How do the baby rabbits look like their mother? How are they different?

The baby rabbits have just been born.

The rabbits are about a week old.

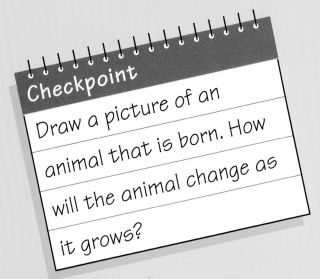

Checkpoint

Draw a picture of an animal that is born. How will the animal change as it grows?

The rabbits are growing and changing.

The rabbit is beginning to look more like the adult.

How does a chicken hatch?

Think about how a caterpillar changes into a butterfly. These changes happen in an order.

The pictures show what happens when a chicken hatches. These things also happen in order.

1. Look at the pictures. In the first picture a chicken is growing inside an egg. What is happening in the second picture?

2. Make a chart like this one.

	How does a chicken hatch?
picture	What is happening?
1	The chicken grows inside the egg.
2	The chicken breaks the shell.
3	
4	

3. The chart shows the first two things that happen when a chicken hatches. Write what is happening in the other pictures.

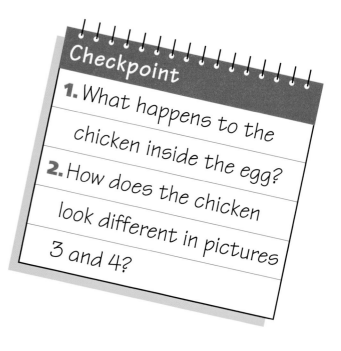

Checkpoint

1. What happens to the chicken inside the egg?

2. How does the chicken look different in pictures 3 and 4?

What did you learn?

Now you know how some animals grow and change. Make a mobile to show what you learned.

You will need: 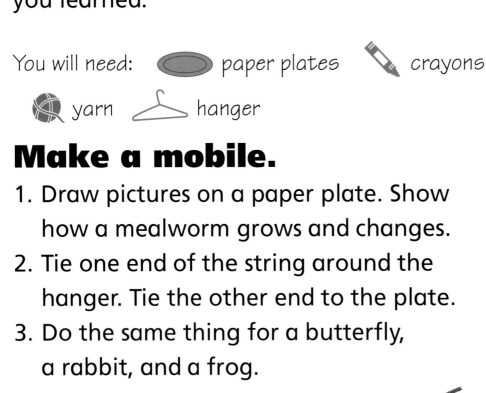 paper plates ✏ crayons yarn ⎁ hanger

Make a mobile.

1. Draw pictures on a paper plate. Show how a mealworm grows and changes.
2. Tie one end of the string around the hanger. Tie the other end to the plate.
3. Do the same thing for a butterfly, a rabbit, and a frog.

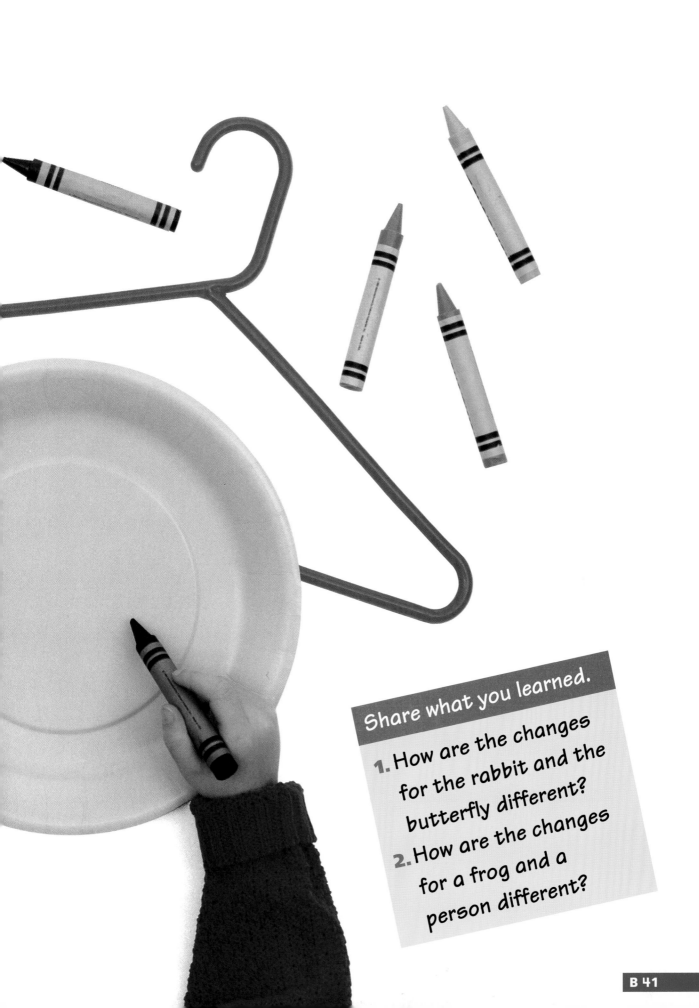

Chapter 3
Changing Things

You know a lot about how living things change. But many other things around you also change. Many things change when you use them. Look at these pictures. Can you find some things that changed?

What things change?

1 Look around your classroom.
2 Find things that change.
3 Make a list of the things you find.
4 Tell how the things change.
5 **Tell about it.** Tell what made the things in your list change.

Ask me what else I want to find out about how things change.

How do you change water?

You know that you can change a lot of things. You even change the water that comes out of your faucet. Look at the pictures to find out how.

What happens to the water after you use it? Water goes through pipes to a place where it is cleaned.

Soap suds and bits of food go down the drain.

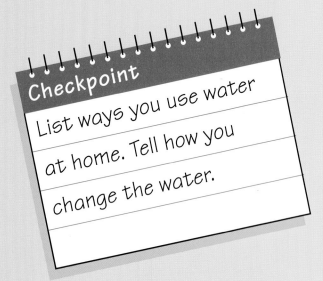

Checkpoint

List ways you use water at home. Tell how you change the water.

Water-color paint goes down the drain.

B 44

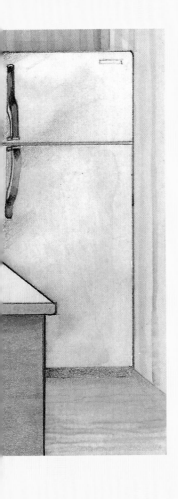

Toothpaste goes down
the drain.

Soap suds and dirt go down
the drain.

How can you clean dirty water?

Dirt and other things can be taken out of water by a filter. Find out how a filter cleans water.

You will need:

 bottle

 screen

 cotton balls

 charcoal

 sand

 tiny stones

 dirty water

Find out about it.

1 Turn the top of the bottle upside down. Put it in the bottom part.

2 Place a piece of screen over the opening.

3 Put the cotton balls on top of the screen. Add the charcoal.

4 Place the sand on top of the charcoal. Then add the stones.

5 Pour the dirty water through your filter.

Write about it.

Make a chart like this one. Write down or draw what you found.

time	how filter looks	how water looks
before filtering		
after filtering		

Checkpoint

1. How did the water change? What changed the water?

2. Take Action! Try to find something else that will filter water.

How do you change land?

Think about things your class throws away. When you throw away trash, you change the land. Read on to find out how.

Most trash is taken to a **landfill.** A landfill is a very big place where trash is buried. Landfills take up a lot of space.

Find things in trash.

You will need: newspapers trash

plastic bags

1. Cover your hands with plastic bags.
2. Cover the floor with newspaper. Empty the trash onto the floor.
3. Look at the different things in the trash. What kinds of things do you find?

Checkpoint

List the things you found in the trash.

How can you use things again?

Think before you throw away that empty box. Is it really trash? Maybe you can reuse it. When you reuse things, less trash goes to landfills.

Reuse means to use something again. Instead of throwing something away, you use it in a different way. The pictures show things that you can reuse. How is each thing being used in a different way?

You can also help reuse things by giving them away. Then someone else can use things you do not use anymore. So think before you throw away a toy. Who else can use it?

B 51

Checkpoint

Tell how something you might throw away can be reused.

How else can you reuse things?

Another way to use things again is to **recycle.** When things are recycled, they are changed. When they are changed, they can be used again.

Metal cans are recycled. The cans are crushed and melted. The recycled metal is used to make new metal things. Maybe you have a toy made of recycled metal.

Sort things to recycle.

You will need: trash 3 cardboard boxes

 3 plastic bags masking tape marker

1. Put a plastic bag inside each cardboard box. Fold the top of the bag over the edges of the box. Tape the bag in place.
2. Write *paper* on one box. Write *plastic* on the second box. Write *metal* on the third box.
3. Put each kind of trash into its box.

Checkpoint

Tell what things you sorted for recycling.

What else can you recycle?

Think about an apple core or a banana peel from your lunch. Food wastes like these can be recycled to make **compost.**

Compost is made mostly from plant wastes. Leaves, grass, and food scraps make good compost. When these things rot, compost forms. Compost can be added to soil to help plants grow.

Make compost.

You will need: plastic jar with cover soil food scraps leaves grass water craft stick

1. Put soil, food scraps, leaves, and grass in the jar.
2. Add a little water. Stir with the craft stick.
3. Cover the jar.
4. Observe the jar every day. How can you tell that the plant wastes are rotting?

Checkpoint

Tell what happens to the plant wastes. How is making compost a way to recycle?

How long does trash stay in a landfill?

You know that most trash is dumped into landfills. But you may not know how long the trash stays there.

Some scientists study trash to find out how old it is. The pictures show four pieces of food found in a landfill.

1. Look at the pictures. The orange peel was about 4 years old when it was found. About how old were the other pieces when they were found?

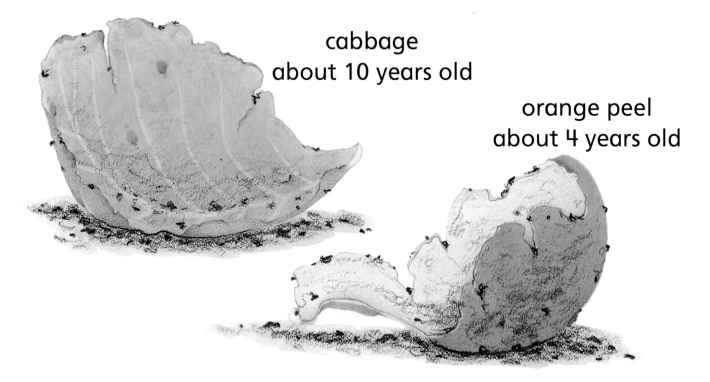

cabbage
about 10 years old

orange peel
about 4 years old

2. Draw a chart like this one.

orange peel										
sausage										
cabbage										
piece of bread										

0 1 2 3 4 5 6 7 8 9 10

years old

3. The chart shows about how old the orange peel was. Color your chart to show about how old each of the other foods were.

bread
about 7 years old

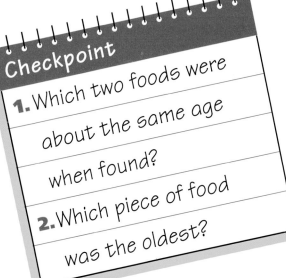

Checkpoint

1. Which two foods were about the same age when found?

2. Which piece of food was the oldest?

sausage
about 4 years old

What did you learn?

You found out how you change things. You learned how to reuse and recycle things. You also learned how to make compost. Now make a mural to show what you learned.

You will need: paper ✏ crayons

Make a mural.

1. Work with a team to plan your mural.
2. Draw things you do that change water.
3. Draw things you do that change land.
4. Draw how you reuse and recycle things.

Share what you learned.

1. What did your mural show about recycling?
2. What can you do so that you make less trash?

A visit to a doctor's office

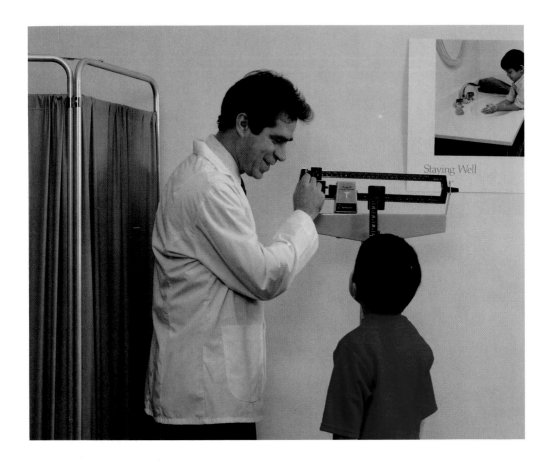

Staying Well

You have probably visited a doctor many times. But today is different. You are here to find out what **nurses** do.

Nurses do things to make sure you are growing. They use a scale to find out what you weigh. Nurses check your heart to see how well it is working. They also give you shots to keep you healthy.

How does a scale work?

3 You use your finger to slide metal weights along the beam.

4 The metal weights balance your weight. The pointer moves to the middle.

2 The beam works like a seesaw. Your weight moves one end down. And the other end moves up.

5 The numbers show your weight.

1 You stand on the scales.

Checkpoint

How does a scale help a nurse know if you are growing?

Show what you know.

You know a lot about how things change. Now you can show what you know. You can make games about things that change. Then you can play your games.

Plan your game.

1. Pick a game to make.
2. What do you need to make your game?
3. How will you play your game?

Play charades.

Make a list of words you learned. Write each word on a note card. Put the cards into a paper bag. Pick a card from the bag. Act out the word. See if your classmates can guess the word. Take turns.

Play a match game.

Draw yourself as a baby on a note card. Draw yourself as an adult on another card. Do the same thing for five different animals. Place all the cards face-down. Play a match game with a partner.

Play a clue game.

Write five sentences that tell how something changes. The sentences will be clues for a partner. Read one clue at a time. Read clues until your partner guesses the thing that changes.

Share what you know.

1. Share your game.
2. Which games did you like playing?
3. What could you add to your game?

Contents

Kids Save Trees

Our classroom trash basket was always full of paper. We knew that trees were cut down to make the paper. We wanted to save some trees. So we decided to use less paper.

We learned a way to make new paper from wastepaper. It was fun to make recycled paper. Here is what we did!

First, we tore some wastepaper into small pieces. We poured warm water on the pieces. After a while, the paper got mushy. Then we stirred the mush with cornstarch.

Next, we spread the paper mush on a screen. We put the screen between the pages of a newspaper. Then we pressed the paper mush to make it flat. We let the paper dry. At last we had recycled paper! We used the paper to make birthday cards.

You can do it.

Think of another way to use less paper. Share your idea with your class.

Kids Get Into Trash

Our class was celebrating Earth Day. We did something special to help the earth. We made a recycling center for our school.

First we got some big boxes. The boxes were for trash. Then we collected trash. We went to every classroom. We filled our boxes with lots of trash.

We collected pieces of chalk and crayons. We collected old notebooks, pens, and pencils. Then we thought of ways to recycle the trash.

Here is how we recycled notebooks. We made note cards from the cardboard covers. The cards are fun to use for art projects. Our teacher saved the wire for science class.

You can do it.

Make a recycling center at home. Show your family how to recycle things.

Kids Make Music

Our class has a box of musical instruments. We have tambourines, triangles, and cymbals. We have sandpaper blocks, bells, and rhythm sticks. But we had no drums, guitars, maracas, or flutes. So we decided to make these musical instruments.

We made instruments from boxes, cans, pans, and jars. We used rubber bands, wax paper, and many other things. Then we decorated our instruments.

When we were finished, we shared our instruments. Each of us played our instrument in different ways. Finally our whole class played our instruments together. We had fun playing our favorite songs. We called our band the Big Bang Band.

You can do it.

Make your own musical instrument from things you find at home. Then use your instrument to play a song.

Kids Play Detective

It was a cold, windy day. We could feel cold air inside our school. The air was coming from outside. But where was the cold air coming in? Our class decided to find out.

We got some straws and strips of plastic wrap. Then we made draft detectors. We used our draft detectors to find drafts.

We looked for drafts in all the classrooms. We checked the library and the lunchroom. We held our draft detectors near windows and doors. When the plastic strips moved, we knew that air was coming in.

We made a map of the places where we found drafts. We showed the map to our school custodian.

You can do it.

Make a draft detector. Use it to find drafts in your home. Tell your family where the drafts are.

Places where we found drafts

window

window

Grade 1 Classroom

door

Answer the questions. Use your own paper.

Chapter 1 Looking at Trees

A 4-5 **1.** Look at the pictures. Which picture shows a tree?

a.  b. 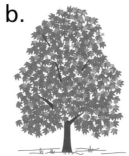 c.

2. Trees can be alike or _____ .

thin   tall   different

A 6-7 **3.** A _____ grows from the trunk of a tree.

seed   leaf   branch

4. The _____ of most trees grow under the ground.

leaves   roots   trunks

A 10-11 **5.** Trees have different _____ .

water   sun   shapes

A 12-13 **6.** Leaves have different sizes and _____ .

branches   shapes   birds

A 14-15 **7.** Needles fall off of trees _____ of the year.

in the fall   at different times   at the end

A 16-17   **8.** A tree ____ grows into a new tree.
needle   branch   seed

9. Some tree seeds are inside a ____ .
covering   root   leaf

Chapter 2 Looking at Plants

A 22-23   **1.** You can even find plants in ____ .
the air   sidewalk cracks   milk

A 24-25   **2.** A tree trunk is a ____ .
leaf   root   stem

3. Leaves and roots are parts of ____ .
plants   needles   trunks

A 26-27   **4.** Look at the picture. Which plant part makes food for the plant?

a. _____

b. ____

c. ____

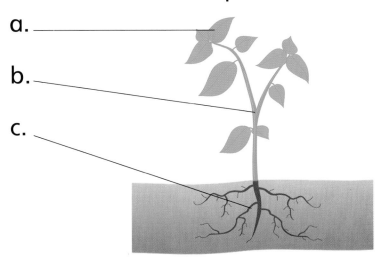

5. A plant cannot live without _____ .

    leaves   fruits   wind

A 28-29   **6.** What plant part holds plants in the soil?

    a. _____

    b. _____

    c. _____

7. Roots take in _____ that the plant needs.

    soil   water   wind

A 30-31   **8.** Stems carry water to the _____ .

    leaves   soil   tubes

9. Roots and stems have _____ that carry water inside of them.

    roots   tubes   soil

A 32-33 **10.** What part of a plant begins to grow from a seed first?

    leaves   stem   roots

11. A baby plant and stored food are parts of a _____ .

    seed   leaf   soil

A 34-35 **12.** Bean seeds grow best in a _____ place.

    cold   warm   pretty

A 36-37 **13.** For plants to grow they need sunlight, air, and _____ .

water   wind   dark

A 38-39 **14.** Different kinds of soil have _____ colors.

the same dark   different

Chapter 3 How Plants Are Used

A 44-45 **1.** Which comes from plants?

paper clips apples   crayons

A 46-47 **2.** People use plants for food and _____ .

clothes   sun   glass

A 48-49 **3.** Look at the pictures. Which shows a root that you can eat?

a.   b.   c.

A 50-51 **4.** Many _____ get food from plants.

animals homes   books

A 52-53 **5.** A _____ can be a home for animals.

seed   tree   pencil

A 54-55 **6.** On a hot day, animals can stay cool in the _____ of a tree.

shade   sunny   seed

Study Guide

Answer the questions. Use your own paper.

Chapter 1 Growing Up

B 4-5

1. You ____ as you grow.

look   change   tell

2. You have ____ since you were a baby.

grown   not changed   become smaller

B 6-7

3. You can ____ in only one year.

smile   change   play

B 8-9

4. Permanent teeth are ____ than first teeth.

whiter   smaller   larger

B 10-11

5. Your size and shape change as you ____ .

grow   play   read

6. Look at the pictures. Which picture shows an adult?

a.   b.   c.

B 12-13

7. You can get rid of some germs by ____ .

eating   washing   running

8. You need to exercise, rest, eat good food, and keep clean so you can ____ .

be healthy   get sick   not grow

B 14-15   **9.** To stay healthy, you should eat more vegetables than _____ .

bread   fruit   fat

10. You should eat more _____ than meat.

a.   b.   c.

B 16-17   **11.** Digestion is the way the body changes _____ you eat.

hair   weight   food

12. In the mouth, a liquid called _____ mixes with food.

water   saliva   ice cream

B 18-19   **13.** The _____ changes food to a soupy liquid.

food tube   stomach   small intestine

Chapter 2 How Animals Grow

B 24-25   **1.** Many animals _____ as they grow.

make   use   change

B 26-27 2. Food, water, a place to live, and ____ are four things animals need to grow.

toys air paper

B 28-29 3. A mealworm is a ____ .

larva beetle pupa

4. Animals called ____ hatch from eggs.

rabbits dogs insects

B 30-31 5. Mealworms can change in size and ____ .

use shape temperature

B 32-33 6. Look at the pictures. Which picture shows a butterfly as it looks when it hatches?

a.

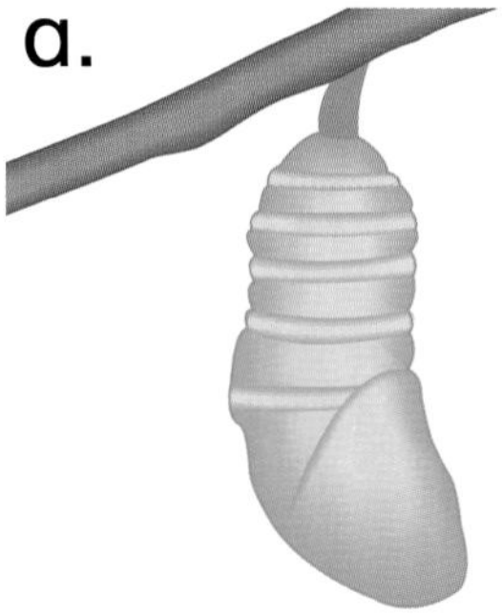

c.

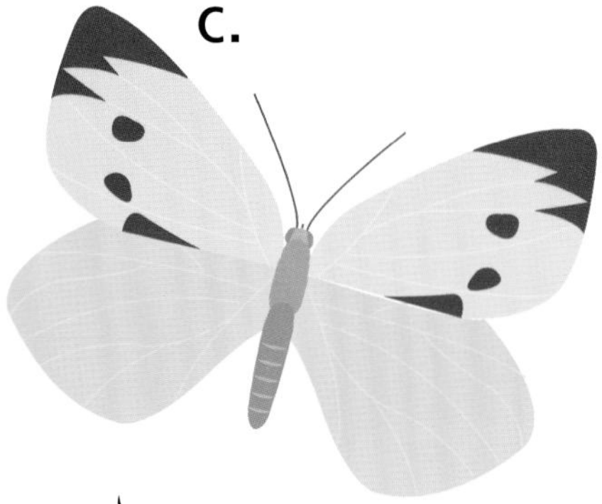

b.

7. A caterpillar changes into a ____ .

pupa covering beetle

B 34-35 8. Which of these animals hatch from eggs?

cats birds horses

9. A baby frog is called a ____ .

larva caterpillar tadpole

B 36-37 10. Cats and dogs grow inside ____ before they are born.

their mothers   eggs   houses

Chapter 3 Changing Things

B 42-43 1. Things change when you ____ them.

use   desk   tree

B 44-45 2. You change water when you ____ .

eat   wash   sleep

B 46-47 3. What can take dirt out of water?

a filter   some soap   more water

B 48-49 4. You change ____ by throwing away trash.

the sky   space   land

B 50-51 5. If you ____ things, less trash will go to landfills.

reuse   throw away   waste

B 52-53 6. Recycled things are changed and ____ .

thrown away   dirtied   used again

B 54-55 7. Look at the pictures. Which one shows things that would make good compost?

a.   b.   c.

Study Guide

Answer the questions. Use your own paper.

Chapter 1 Hearing and Seeing

C 4-5 **1.** Sounds may be alike or _____ .

different   colorful   hard

C 6-7 **2.** Sounds can be loud or soft, high or _____ .

low   dark   blue

C 8-9 **3.** If you pluck a rubber band hard, the rubber band makes a _____ sound.

soft   light   loud

C 10-11 **4.** Sounds that are _____ can hurt your ears.

soft   low   loud

C 12-13 **5.** Look at the picture. Which part of the ear is the eardrum?

a.

b.

c.

6. You hear sounds when sound messages reach the _____ .

brain   path   outer ear

C 14-15 **7.** It is easier to tell where sounds come from with _____ .

two ears   your eyes   one ear

C 16-17 **8.** You need ____ to see.

a nose   darkness   light

C 18-19 **9.** Look at the picture. Which part of the eye is the pupil?

a.

b.

c.

C 20-21 **10.** It is easier to catch a ball when you ____ .

use two eyes close your eyes use one eye

Chapter 2 Making Sounds

C 26-27 **1.** When you pluck a rubber band to make a sound, the rubber band ____ .

moves back and forth   stays still   breaks

C 28-29 **2.** When objects move back and forth quickly, they ____ .

break   vibrate   bend

3. When objects vibrate, they make ____ .

rubber bands   smiles   sounds

C 30-31 **4.** Sound can ____ through objects.

travel   play   see

5. Sound can be heard best when it travels through ____ .

wood   water   air

C 32-33 **6.** Sound travels through the air ____ .

only up   in all directions   only down

7. You hear sound through air because sound makes air ____ .

vibrate   stop   warm

C 34-35 **8.** A string telephone shows you that sound travels ____ .

lightly   through a string   slowly

C 36-37 **9.** The ____ of your ear is good for catching sounds.

size and shape   color   trumpet

C 38-39 **10.** The sounds of different instruments ____ to make music.

shine   come together   march

11. Look at the picture. Which part of the drum vibrates the most when you play it?

a. ____

b. ____

c. ____

Chapter 3 Light

C 44-45 1. Light travels in a _____ .

    straight line   wavy line   circle

C 46-47 2. Light _____ move through a wall.

    can   can not   always will

3. Light is stopped by _____ .

    plastic wrap   wood   air

C 48-49 4. When light _____ through an object, a shadow forms.

    can not go   travels   moves

C 50-51 5. Light bounces best when it hits _____ objects.

    rough, dark   smooth, shiny   smooth, dark

C 52-53 6. Look at the pictures. Which one shows that water can make objects look different?

a.   b.   c.

C 54-55 7. Light is made up of _____ .

    one color   no color   many colors

Study Guide

Answer the questions. Use your own paper.

Chapter 1 Describing Weather

D 4-5   **1.** Which word tells about weather?

cloudy   travel   hard

D 6-7   **2.** Weather can ____ during the day.

chart   stop   change

D 8-9   **3.** The ____ tells how warm the air is.

tube   temperature   wind

4. You can find the temperature of air by using a ____ .

flag   rain gauge   thermometer

5. As air gets warmer, the liquid inside a thermometer moves ____ .

down   sideways   up

D 10-11   **6.** Another name for moving air is ____ .

temperature   wind   flag

D 12-13   **7.** Look at the pictures. In which picture is the wind blowing hardest?

a.   b.   c.

D 14-15 **8.** A tool you can use to measure rainfall is called a ____ .

rain gauge   rain cap   thermometer

D 16-17 **9.** During a thunderstorm you usually see dark clouds, rain, and ____ .

snow   lightning   sunshine

Chapter 2 Air, Water, and Weather

D 22-23 **1.** You cannot see ____ , but it is all around.

rain   sun   air

D 24-25 **2.** Look at the pictures. Which picture shows that there is water in the air?

a.   b.   c.

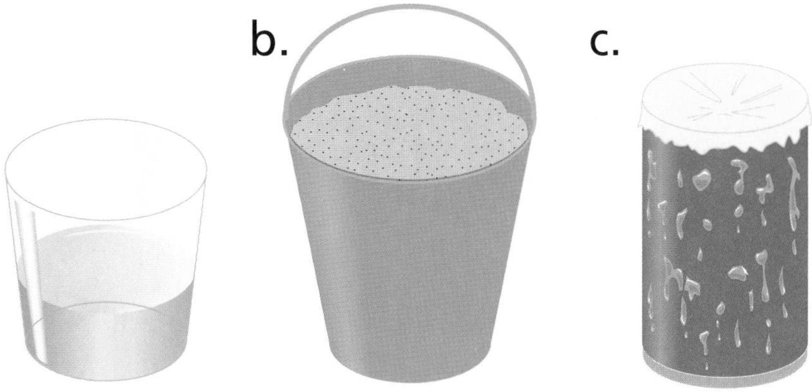

D 26-27 **3.** Water that is in the air is called ____ .

water vapor   cool water   wet water

4. When water vapor ____ , it changes to liquid water.

evaporates   heats   condenses

D 28-29 **5.** Puddles dry up after all the water ____ .

evaporates   condenses   gets cold

6. When liquid water evaporates, it changes to _____ .

rain water vapor a puddle

D 30-31 **7.** Puddles will dry quickly on a _____ day.

rainy cold windy

D 32-33 **8.** Water evaporates faster in the _____ .

shade sun winter

D 34-35 **9.** When water vapor moves high in the sky, it cools and _____ .

condenses evaporates forms a puddle

D 36-37 **10.** Look at the pictures. What forms when water vapor condenses?

a. b. c.

D 38-39 **11.** Water moves from clouds to the earth and back to clouds again in the _____ .

rain water cycle storm

D 40-41 **12.** When do you see clouds that look like feathers?

in a storm on rainy days on sunny days

Chapter 3 Weather and You

D 46-47 **1.** Knowing about weather helps you choose what to ____ .

wear   say   eat

D 48-49 **2.** When the weather is ____ , you might play in the shade.

cold and snowy   sunny and hot   rainy

3. Look at the picture. What kind of weather is this child dressed for?

cold and snowy   warm and sunny   rainy

D 50-51 **4.** In cold weather, a coat keeps you ____ .
cold   wet   warm

D 52-53 **5.** Wear ____ colors to stay warm on a cold, sunny day.

light   dark   pretty

6. To stay cool, what is the best color to wear on a hot, sunny day?
yellow   black   white

D 54-55 **7.** A ____ is a time of year.
clock   season   weather

Scientists like to learn about the world. They like to help with problems. They use scientific methods to find answers. Scientists use many steps in their methods. Sometimes they use the steps in different ways. You can use these steps to do experiments.

Explain the Problem

Ask a question like this. Does sound travel?

Make Observations

Tell about the size, color, or shape
of things.

Give a Hypothesis

Try to answer the problem. Tell your idea.
Then do the experiment.

Make a Chart or Graph

Tell what you saw in your chart or graph.

Make Conclusions

Decide if your hypothesis is right or wrong.

Safety in Science

Scientists are careful when they do experiments. You need to be careful too. Here are some rules to remember.

- Read each experiment carefully.

- Wear cover goggles when needed.

- Clean up spills right away.

- Never taste or smell unknown things.

- Do not shine lights in someone's eyes.

- Put things away when you are done.

- Wash your hands after each experiment.

Experiment with Plants and Light

Brad is watering his plants. One plant is bent. It is leaning toward the window. Brad thinks the plant is bending toward light. He wonders if other plants bend toward light.

Problem

Do some plants bend toward light?

Give Your Hypothesis

Answer the problem.
Then do the experiment.

Follow the Directions

1 Make a chart like this one.

time	bends toward light
after 1 week	
1 week after turning plant	

2 Put a small plant near a sunny window for one week.

3 Does the plant bend toward light? Write yes or no in your chart.

4 Turn the plant so it bends away from the window. Leave it for 1 week.

5 Write in your chart if the plant bends.

Tell Your Conclusion

Do some plants bend toward light?

Experiment with Brushing

Jack rinses his mouth after lunch. This makes his mouth feel clean. He wonders why he needs to brush. Can just water clean his teeth? Jack wonders if brushing cleans better than just rinsing.

Problem

Does brushing help make things clean?

Give Your Hypothesis

Answer the problem.
Then do the experiment.

Follow the Directions

1 Make a chart like this one.

how I cleaned spoon	Is spoon clean?
rinsing	
brushing	

2 Rub peanut butter on 2 spoons. Let the spoons sit for 2 hours.

3 Run water over 1 spoon. Does rinsing help clean the spoon?

4 Scrub the other spoon with a brush.

5 Does brushing help clean the spoon? Write your answers in your chart.

6 Circle in the chart which way cleans better.

Tell Your Conclusion

Does brushing help make things clean?

Experiment with Color

Debra just became a crossing guard. She brought home her orange belt. Her brother Matt thinks orange is ugly. He likes blue.

Matt wonders why the belts are orange or yellow. He notices that the school bus also is yellow. He wonders if yellow is easy to see.

Problem

Is it easier to see yellow than blue?

Give Your Hypothesis

Answer the problem.
Then do the experiment.

Follow the Directions

1 Make a chart like this one.

color	easy to see
yellow	
blue	

2 Get a piece of bright yellow paper.
Tape it against a gray paper.
Can you see the yellow easily?
Write the answer in your chart.

3 Then get a piece of blue paper. Tape
it against the gray paper. Can you
see the blue easily? Fill in your chart.

4 Which color is easier to see?
Circle the color in your chart.

Tell Your Conclusion

Is it easier to see yellow than blue?

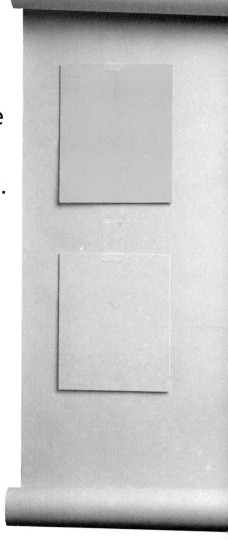

Experiment with a Thermometer

Kim and Mary are walking home from school. They take off their coats. They needed their coats this morning. It was cool then. Now it is warm. Kim and Mary think the air gets warmer during the day.

Problem

Can air get warmer during the day?

Give Your Hypothesis

Answer the problem.
Then do the experiment.

Follow the Directions

1 Make a chart like this one.

time	temperature
morning	
afternoon	

2 Put a thermometer outside.

3 Read the temperature in the morning.

4 Read the temperature in the afternoon.

5 Read the temperature in the morning and afternoon for 2 days.

6 When is the temperature highest? When is it lowest? Write your answers in your chart. Circle which time of day is warmer.

Tell Your Conclusion
Can air get warmer during the day?

A **adult,** p. B10, An adult is a living thing that is full grown.

B **baby plant,** p. A30, A baby plant is on the inside of a seed. Baby plants can grow into adult plants.

bark, p. A52, Bark covers the trunk and branches of trees.

beetle, p. B28, A beetle is an insect with two shiny front wings. The front wings cover the two back wings when the beetle is not flying.

brain, p. C12, The brain is a part of the body that is inside the head. The brain helps people think, feel, move, see, and hear.

branch, p. A6, A branch is the part of a tree that grows out from the trunk.

broad leaf, p. A14, A broad leaf is a leaf that is flat.

butterfly, p. B32, A butterfly is an insect. Butterflies have four wings that have bright colors.

C **caterpillar,** p. B32, A caterpillar is the larva of a butterfly or moth. Some caterpillars look like furry, colorful worms.

change, p. B4, Change means to become different.

compost, p. B54, Compost is a mixture of plant waste that rots. Compost can be added to soil to help plants grow.

condense, p. D26, Condense means to change from water vapor to liquid water.

cotton, p. A46, Cotton is a plant. People make clothes from cotton plants.

coverings, p. A16, A covering is something that covers the seed. The seed covering keeps the seed safe until it can grow into a new plant.

D **digestion,** p. B16, Digestion changes food so that the body can use it.

E **eardrum,** p. C12, The eardrum is the skin at the end of the tunnel in the ear. The eardrum moves when sound hits it.

evaporate, p. D28, Evaporate means to change from liquid water to water vapor.

exercise, p. B12, Exercise is moving your body to stay healthy. Running, swimming, and playing ball are kinds of exercise.

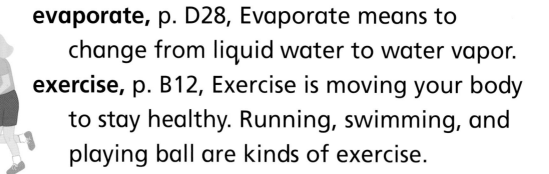

F **filter,** p. B46, A filter is used to take dirt out of water, other liquids, or air.

first teeth, p. B8, First teeth are the teeth people get when they are babies.

flower, p. A25, A flower is the part of a plant that makes seeds.

food tube, p. B18, The food tube is a part of the body. Food goes from the mouth to the stomach through the food tube.

G **germ,** p. B13, A germ is very tiny and can be seen only with a microscope. Germs can make you sick.

group, p. A12, A group is a set of objects that are alike in some way.

H **hatch,** p. B28, Hatch means to come out of an egg.

healthy, p. B12, Healthy means to be well, or not sick.

I

inner ear parts, p. C12, Inner ear parts are the parts that are inside the head. The inner ear parts send sound messages to the brain.

insect, p. B28, An insect is a very small animal. Insects have three body parts and six legs.

instrument, p. C38, An instrument is something that makes music.

L

landfill, p. B48, A landfill is a large place where trash is buried.

larva, p. B28, A larva is the insect form that hatches from an egg. The larva often looks like a worm.

leaf, p. A6, A leaf is a part of a plant. Leaves make food for the plant.

lens, p. C19, The lens is the clear part of the eye. The lens is behind the pupil.

light, p. C42, Light comes from the sun, flashlights, and other things.

lumber, p. A56, Lumber is wood that is cut into boards.

mealworm, p. B25, A mealworm is the larva of a beetle.

needle, p. A14, A needle is a leaf that is thin and pointed.

noise, p. C10, Noise is sound that you do not like to hear. Loud noises can sometimes hurt your ears.

permanent teeth, p. B8, Permanent teeth are the new teeth that grow in when a person's first teeth fall out.

plant, p. A22, A plant is a living thing. Most plants can make their own food from sunlight, air, and water.

pupa, p. B28, A pupa is the form of an insect that the larva changes into. The pupa changes into an adult.

pupil, p. C19, The pupil is the opening in the center of the eye. Light enters the eye through the pupil.

R **rain gauge,** p. D14, A rain gauge is used to measure how much rain falls.

rainfall, p. D14, Rainfall is how much rain, snow, or sleet fall.

recycle, p. B52, Recycle means to change something so that it can be used again.

rest, p. B12, Rest is being still or quiet, or sleeping.

reuse, p. B50, Reuse means to use something, such as a lunch bag, again.

root, p. A7, A root is a part of a plant. Roots hold plants in the ground.

rot, p. B54, Rot means to break down or to become spoiled.

S **saliva,** p. B16, Saliva is a liquid in the mouth. Saliva helps to digest food.

season, p. D54, A season is one of the four parts of the year. The seasons are spring, summer, fall, and winter.

seed, p. A16, A seed is the part of a plant that grows into a new plant. Seeds are made in flowers.

seed coat, p. A30, A seed coat is the outside part of a seed.

shade, p. A54, Shade is a place that is not in bright sunlight. Shady places are cooler than sunny places.

shadow, p. C48, A shadow is a dark shape that is made when an object blocks light.

small intestine, p. B18, The small intestine is a long, winding tube in the body. The small intestine changes food so that the body can use it.

soil, p. A38, Soil is the top layer of the earth. Plants grow in soil.

sort, p. A12, Sort means to put together things that are alike.

sound, p. C4, A sound is something you hear. A sound is made when an object vibrates.

stem, p. A24, A stem is the main part of a plant. Stems hold plants up and carry water and food to other plant parts.

stomach, p. B18, The stomach is a part of the body. The stomach changes food into a soupy liquid.

stored food, p. A30, Stored food is inside a seed. The baby plant uses the stored food to start growing.

tadpole, p. B35, A tadpole is a very young frog or toad. Tadpoles have tails and live only in water.

temperature, p. D8, Temperature is a measurement of how hot or cold something is.

thermometer, p. D8, A thermometer is used to measure temperature.

thunderstorm, p. D16, A thunderstorm is a kind of weather that has strong winds, heavy rain, lightning, and thunder.

tree, p. A4, A tree is a large plant with a trunk, branches, and leaves.

trunk, p. A6, A trunk is the stem of a tree.

tube, p. A28, The tubes in plant roots and stems carry water or food.

tunnel, p. C13, A tunnel leads from the outside of the ear to the eardrum. Sounds move through the tunnel.

V **vibrate,** p. C28, Vibrate means to move back and forth very quickly.

W **waste,** p. B54, Waste is something that has been thrown away.

water cycle, p. D38, The water cycle is the movement of water between the air and the earth.

water vapor, p. D26, Water vapor is a form of water in the air. When liquid water evaporates, it changes to water vapor.

weather, p. D4, Weather is what the air outside is like. The air may be still or windy, hot or cold, wet or dry.

wind, p. D10, Wind is moving air.

wood, p. A47, Wood is the hard part of the trunk and branches of a tree.

Acknowledgments

ScottForesman

Editorial: Terry Flohr, Janet Helenthal, Carl Benoit, Mary Ann Mortellaro, Mary Jayne Horgan, Dorothy Murray, Camille Salerno, Linda Roach, Denise Fitzsimmons

Art and Design: Barbara Schneider, Jacqueline Kolb

Picture Research/Photo Studio: Nina Page, Karen Koblik, John Moore, Phoebe Novak

Production: Barbara Albright, Francine Simon

Marketing: Ed Rock

Outside Credits
Interior Design
Kym Abrams Design, Inc.
The Quarasan Group, Inc.

Unless otherwise acknowledged, all photographs are the property of Scott, Foresman and Company. Page abbreviations are as follows: **(T)** top, **(C)** center, **(B)** bottom, **(L)** left, **(R)** right, **(INS)** inset.

Module A
Photographs
Front & Back Cover: Background: John Shaw/Bruce Coleman, Inc.   Children's Photos: Michael Goss for Scott, Foresman and Company.

Page A4(L) Zig Leszczynski/EARTH SCENES **A4-A5** John Eastcott/YVA Momatiuk/The Image Works **A5(L)** E.R.Degginger **A5(R)** Susan McCartney/ Photo Researchers, Inc. **A8(T)** R.F.Head/EARTH SCENES **A8(B)** Grant Heilman Photography **A9(TL)** E.R.Degginger **A9(TR)** William E.Ferguson **A9(B)** John Shaw/ Bruce Coleman, Inc. **A10(L&R)** John Shaw/Bruce Coleman, Inc. **A10(C)** E.R.Degginger **A30** Willard Clay Photography **A46** Jean-Claude Carton/Bruce Coleman, Inc. **A54** H.Confer/The Image Works **A60** Mark Burnett/Stock Boston

Illustrations
Page A2 Jan Palmer **A6-7** Lois Leonard Stock **A18-19** Jan Palmer **A22-23** Diana Philbrook **A24-25** Erika Kors **A28** Ebet Dudley **A32** Erika Kors **A36-37** Ilene Robinette **A40-41** Linda Hawkins **A52-53** Cindy Brodie **A55** Jan Palmer **A61** Mike Eagle

Module B
Photographs
Front & Back Cover: Background: E.R.Degginger   Children's Photos: Michael Goss for Scott, Foresman and Company.

Page B2 Ron Rovtar/FPG **B3** John Shaw/Tom Stack & Associates **B4-B5** Luann Benoit **B6(T)** Ron Rovtar/FPG **B13(T)** Brent Jones/ Tony Stone Worldwide **B24(L)** Larry Lefever/Grant Heilman Photography **B24(R)** Thomas Howland/Grant Heilman Photography **B24(T)** Barry L.Runk/Grant Heilman Photography **B25(B)** Sonia Wasco/Grant Heilman Photography **B26-B27** Stephen J.Krasemann/DRK Photo **B32(L&R) & B33** John Shaw/Tom Stack & Associates **B34** E.R.Degginger **B48** Willie L.Hill

Illustrations
Page B9 Ka Botzis **B14** Deborah Morse **B18** Deborah Morse **B20** Deborah Morse **B28-29** Laurie O'Keefe **B35** Lois Leonard Stock **B36-37** Edward Brooks **B38-39** Lois Leonard Stock **B42-43** Andrea Z. Tachiera **B44-45** Susan Spellman **B56-57** Nancy Lee Walter **B61** Mike Eagle

Module C
Photographs
Front & Back Cover: Background: Gary A.Conner/PhotoEdit Children's Photos: Michael Goss for Scott, Foresman and Company.

Page C2 L.L.T.Rhodes/ EARTH SCENES **C3** E.R.Degginger **C6** Thomas Wanstall/The Image Works **C7(L)** John Cancalosi/ Peter Arnold, Inc. **C7(R)** Don & Pat Valenti **C10** L.L.T.Rhodes/ EARTH SCENES **C36** The Bettmann Archive **C52(B)** E.R.Degginger **C53(T)** CoCo McCoy/Rainbow **C54** Runk/Schoenberger/Grant Heilman Photography **C55** E.R.Degginger

Illustrations
Page C4-5 Meryl Henderson **C12-13** Deborah Morse **C18-19** Deborah Morse **C22-23** Ebet Dudley **C26-27** Roberta Polfus **C32-33** Ilene Robinette **C40** Lisa Pompelli **C61** Mike Eagle

Module D
Photographs
Front & Back Cover: Background: Tom Bean/DRK Photo Children's Photos: Michael Goss for Scott, Foresman and Company.

Page D2 Jeff Persons/Stock Boston **D6** Jerry Howard/Stock Boston **D10** Tony Arruza/Bruce Coleman, Inc. **D16(L)** Bruce Davidson/EARTH SCENES **D16(R)** Barry Parker/Bruce Coleman, Inc. **D17(L)** R.F.Myers/Visuals Unlimited **D17(R)** S.Savino/The Image Works **D22-D23** Joseph A.DiChello **D27** Garv Griffen/ANIMALS ANIMALS **D36** James Tallon **D39** Stephen J.Krasemann/DRK Photo **D40-D41** David R.Frazier **D41(T)** Tom Bean/DRK Photo **D41(B)** Charlton Photographs **D46-47** Ben Simmons/Stock Market **D48** Bob Daemmrich/Tony Stone Worldwide **D49** Jeff Persons/Stock Boston **D60** Brownie Harris/The Stock Market

Illustrations
Page D2 Linda Hawkins **D3** Susan Spellman **D4-5** Andrea Z. Tachiera **D8** Linda Hawkins **D12-13** Ted Carr **D18** Judy Sakaguchi **D28** Susan Spellman **D32-33** Rondi Collette **D42-43** Sharron O'Neil **D54-55** Jan Palmer **D56-57** Nancy Lee Walter **D61** Mike Eagle

Back Matter
Illustrations
Pages 10-25, 38-46 Precision Graphics